I GOT 95 THESES

By Martin Luther and
Johann Tetzel

With additional thoughts
by Josh Hamon

First Printing: 2019
ISBN 978-1-7339650-0-2
Published by The Ministry of War
Bremerton, WA 98310
TheMinistryofWar.com

Ordering Information:
Special discounts are available on quantity purchases by corporations, associations, educators and others. For details email hello@TheMinistryofWar.com.

U.S. trade bookstores and wholesalers:
Please contact hello@TheMinistryofWar.com.

out of **love**
for the **truth**

INTRODUCTION

If your instinct is to read the 95 Theses with reverence or contempt, you are missing the point. There are billions of people today who call themselves Christians and a list of what they agree on could fit on a grain of rice. The 95 Theses is an important historical document and should be viewed as such. Today, its value is not in its theology but in its place in history.

Approach it honestly.

Approach it with fresh eyes. It is okay for people to have questions. If you believe in an objective reality, then let the 95 Theses stands on its own.

The following pages are the work of Martin Luther, some initial responses of Johann Tetzel, and my[*] comments and annotations. My goal is to bring you history in a fresh way because I believe deeply in the beauty of Truth. History is. Even if that makes people uncomforatble. If you hear something new or unexpected, don't take it at face value and don't discard it at face value. Do additional research, think and test.

And maybe enjoy it?

First up is Martin Luther's 95 Theses, the work that started the Protestant Reformation. It is 95 statements that Luther wanted to debate. The theses concern the Pope's authority, especially in the matter of indulgences.

------

* mostly sarcastic

At the most basic level, an indulgence is the remission of the penalities connected to a sin. The earliest recorded plenary (complete) indulgence was in 1095 by Pope Urban II. Over the the last thousand years, a lot has changed around indulgences, in Luther's day he felt they had gone from the removing the earthly penalties to offering people full salvation before God. So he wanted to debate the limits of indulgences.

To modern eyes, the 95 Theses can be a difficult read. However, with a little structural analysis, you will be able to better understand the intended flow:

- Theses 1 through 4 are the Luther's propositions (his assumptions.)
- 5 is the heart of the document. If Luther had social media, this is the thesis he would have posted.
- In theses 5 through 20, he discusses the limits of papal authority over indulgences. This is where he gets into trouble with the Catholic Church at large.
- Theses 21 through 41 are a three-pronged attack on the abuse of the indulgence preachers.
  - 21 through 24 question the idea that indulgences can release someone from all sin.
  - 25 through 29 examine the pope's power over souls in Purgatory.
  - 30 through 41 examines the relationship between contrition and indulgences.
- "What Christians should be taught" is made up of theses 42 through 55. The same style will be used almost exclusively in Tetzel's second disputation. While theses 5 is the heart of the document, these theses are central as well.

- Theses 56 through 68 discuss the premise that the power of indulgences is said to come from the teasury of merits. Luther asserts that the treasury of merits is too vague.
- Beyond the indulgence preachers, Luther examines the role of the rest of the clergy in regard to idulgences in theses 69 through 80.
- Before closing, in theses 81 through 91 Luther takes time to assume some objections and rebutts them.
- Luther's conclusion consists of the final four theses.

A disputation (debate) was held the following January, but not with Luther in attendance. There, Johann Tetzel presented two works he developed as a response to Luther. At the time, Luther was an Augustinian monk and Tetzel was a Dominican, which might have been the reason Luther wasn't invited. These documents are the *First Disputation of Johann Tetzel* and the *Second Disputation of Johann Tetzel.*

It is widely believed that the *First Disputation of Johann Tetzel* was authored by Conrad Wimpina. In his life Tetzel denies many things that were attributed to him, most notably the jingle in thesis 27 often paraphrased as "As soon as the coin in the coffer rings, the soul from purgatory flings." and thesis 75, which I'll let you read for yourself. However, Tetzel does not contest his name on this document by Wimpina.

The *First Disputation of Johann Tetzel* is not an exciting read, as it mostly just says that Luther erred. I have published it here because it is part of the historical record. While Luther's 95 Theses were reprinted many times, it is no surprise that the first disputation did not get the same attention. For those of you keeping score at home, the first disputation did not dispute the following theses by Luther: 12, 17, 38, 45, 51, 57, 63-65, 68, 70, 71, 73, 74, 78-80, and 90-95.

The *Second Disputation of Johann Tetzel* is a more robust document. Presented as 50 statements almost exclusively following the "Christians should be taught" mantra that Luther employed, the second disputation goes into greater detail about the current stance of the Catholic Church.

When Luther published his work, his goal was to discuss what he felt were abuses in the indulgence system, however, people read it as a document attacking the authority of the pope. Over the next couple of years, Luther would attend several disputations and Imperial Diets and would see a great schism in the church. The world would never be the same.

Please enjoy responsibly.

A few additional citation notes for the +1 nerds in the crowd. The first and second disputations were translated by Mr. John Keesee Goode, class of 1901, and have been further revised and annotated by Professor Vedder of the Crozer Theological Seminary.

This translation of the 95 Theses into English can be found at archive.org.

MARTIN LUTHER 95 THESES

DISPUTATION OF DOCTOR MARTIN LUTHER ON
THE POWER AND EFFICACY OF INDULGENCES

OCTOBER 31, 1517

Out of love for the truth and the desire to bring it to light,

the following propositions will be discussed at Wittenberg, under the presidency of the Reverend Father Martin Luther, Master of Arts and of Sacred Theology, and Lecturer in Ordinary on the same at that place. Wherefore he requests that those who are unable to be present and debate orally with us, may do so by letter.

In the Name our Lord Jesus Christ. Amen.

1

Our Lord and Master Jesus Christ, when He said *Poenitentiam agite,*[*] willed that the whole life of believers should be repentance.

2

This word cannot be understood to mean sacramental penance, i.e., confession and satisfaction, which is administered by the priests.

---

[*] This can be translated as "repent" (usually by Protestants), "penitence" and "do penance" (usually by Catholics.)

3

Yet it means not inward repentance only; nay, there is no inward repentance which does not outwardly work divers[*] mortifications of the flesh.

4

The penalty [of sin], therefore, continues so long as hatred of self continues; for this is the true inward repentance, and continues until our entrance into the kingdom of heaven.

---

* In modern times, we would add an 'e.' Diverse mortifications of flesh or repentence reveals itself inwardly and outwardly.

5*

The pope does not intend to remit, and cannot remit any penalties other than those which he has imposed either by his own authority or by that of the canons.

---

* Here we have the core of the 95 Theses. Initially Luther was looking to fight indulgence preachers, not the pope. Many others didn't read it that way, including the pope.

6

The pope cannot remit any guilt, except by declaring that it has been remitted by God and by assenting to God's remission; though, to be sure, he may grant remission in cases reserved to his judgment. If his right to grant remission in such cases were despised, the guilt would remain entirely unforgiven.

7

God remits guilt to no one whom He does not, at the same time, humble in all things and bring into subjection to His vicar, the priest.

8

The penitential canons* are imposed only on the living, and, according to them, nothing should be imposed on the dying.

---

* Penitential canons is jargony way to say religious rules

9

Therefore the Holy Spirit in the pope is kind to us, because in his decrees he always makes exception of the article of death and of necessity.

10

Ignorant and wicked are the doings of those priests who, in the case of the dying, reserve canonical penances for purgatory.*

---

* Or "it's a jerk move to add time to purgatory instead of allowing penance now."

11

This changing of the canonical penalty to the penalty of purgatory is quite evidently one of the tares that were sown while the bishops slept.

12

In former times the canonical penalties were imposed not after, but before absolution, as tests of true contrition.

13

The dying are freed by death from all penalties; they are already dead to canonical rules, and have a right to be released from them.

14

The imperfect health [of soul], that is to say, the imperfect love, of the dying brings with it, of necessity, great fear; and the smaller the love, the greater is the fear.

15

This fear and horror is sufficient of itself alone (to say nothing of other things) to constitute the penalty of purgatory, since it is very near to the horror of despair.

16

Hell, purgatory, and heaven seem to differ as do despair, almost-despair, and the assurance of safety.

17

With souls in purgatory it seems necessary that horror should grow less and love increase.

18

It seems unproved, either by reason or Scripture, that they are outside the state of merit, that is to say, of increasing love.

19

Again, it seems unproved that they, or at least that all of them, are certain or assured of their own blessedness, though we may be quite certain of it.

20

Therefore by "full remission of all penalties" the pope means not actually "of all," but only of those imposed by himself.

21

Therefore those preachers of indulgences are in error, who say that by the pope's indulgences a man is freed from every penalty, and saved;

22

Whereas he remits to souls in purgatory no penalty which, according to the canons, they would have had to pay in this life.

23

If it is at all possible to grant to any one the remission of all penalties whatsoever, it is certain that this remission can be granted only to the most perfect, that is, to the very fewest.

24

It must needs be, therefore, that the greater part of the people are deceived by that indiscriminate and highsounding promise of release from penalty.

25

The power which the pope has, in a general way, over purgatory, is just like the power which any bishop or curate has, in a special way, within his own diocese or parish.

26

The pope does well when he grants remission to souls [in purgatory], not by the power of the keys (which he does not possess), but by way of intercession.

27

They preach vanity who say that so soon as the penny jingles into the money-box, the soul flies out [of purgatory].

28

It is certain that when the penny jingles into the money-box, gain and avarice can be increased, but the result of the intercession of the Church is in the power of God alone.

29

Who knows whether all the souls in purgatory wish to be brought out of it, as in the legend of Sts. Severinus and Paschal.*

30

No one is sure that his own contrition is sincere; much less that he has attained full remission.

---

* This refers to two Saints who wished to stay in purgatory so they could suffer on behalf of others.

31

Rare as is the man that is truly penitent, so rare is also the man who truly buys indulgences, i.e., such men are most rare.

32

They will be condemned eternally, together with their teachers, who believe themselves sure of their salvation because they have letters of pardon.

33

Men must be on their guard against those who say that the pope's pardons are that inestimable gift of God by which man is reconciled to Him.

34

For these "graces of pardon" concern only the penalties of sacramental satisfaction, and these are appointed by man.

35

They preach no Christian doctrine who teach that contrition is not necessary in those who intend to buy souls out of purgatory or to buy confessionalia.

36

Every truly repentant Christian has a right to full remission of penalty and guilt, even without letters of pardon.

37

Every true Christian, whether living or dead, has part in all the blessings of Christ and the Church; and this is granted him by God, even without letters of pardon.

38

Nevertheless, the remission and participation [in the blessings of the Church] which are granted by the pope are in no way to be despised, for they are, as I have said, the declaration of divine remission.

39

It is most difficult, even for the very keenest theologians, at one and the same time to commend to the people the abundance of pardons and [the need of] true contrition.

40

True contrition seeks and loves penalties, but liberal pardons only relax penalties and cause them to be hated, or at least, furnish an occasion [for hating them].

41

Apostolic pardons are to be preached with caution, lest the people may falsely think them preferable to other good works of love.

42*

Christians are to be taught that the pope does not intend the buying of pardons to be compared in any way to works of mercy.

---

* "Christians are to be taught" is a phrase that will be featured here in the 95 Theses and in Tetzel's 2nd disputation.

43

Christians are to be taught that he who gives to the poor or lends to the needy does a better work than buying pardons;

44

Because love grows by works of love, and man becomes better; but by pardons man does not grow better, only more free from penalty.

45

Christians are to be taught that he who sees a man in need, and passes him by, and gives [his money] for pardons, purchases not the indulgences of the pope, but the indignation of God.

46

Christians are to be taught that unless they have more than they need, they are bound to keep back what is necessary for their own families, and by no means to squander it on pardons.

47

Christians are to be taught that the buying of pardons is a matter of free will, and not of commandment.

48

Christians are to be taught that the pope, in granting pardons, needs, and therefore desires, their devout prayer for him more than the money they bring.

49

Christians are to be taught that the pope's pardons are useful, if they do not put their trust in them; but altogether harmful, if through them they lose their fear of God.

50

Christians are to be taught that if the pope knew the exactions of the pardon-preachers, he would rather that St. Peter's Church should go to ashes, than that it should be built up with the skin, flesh and bones of his sheep.

51

Christians are to be taught that it would be the pope's wish, as it is his duty, to give of his own money to very many of those from whom certain hawkers of pardons cajole money, even though the church of St. Peter might have to be sold.

52

The assurance of salvation by letters of pardon is vain, even though the commissary, nay, even though the pope himself, were to stake his soul upon it.

53

They are enemies of Christ and of the pope, who bid the Word of God be altogether silent in some Churches, in order that pardons may be preached in others.

54

Injury is done the Word of God when, in the same sermon, an equal or a longer time is spent on pardons than on this Word.

55

It must be the intention of the pope that if pardons, which are a very small thing, are celebrated with one bell, with single processions and ceremonies, then the Gospel, which is the very greatest thing, should be preached with a hundred bells, a hundred processions, a hundred ceremonies.

56

The "treasures of the Church," out of which the pope grants indulgences, are not sufficiently named or known among the people of Christ.

57

That they are not temporal treasures is certainly evident, for many of the vendors do not pour out such treasures so easily, but only gather them.

58

Nor are they the merits of Christ and the Saints, for even without the pope, these always work grace for the inner man, and the cross, death, and hell for the outward man.

59

St. Lawrence said that the treasures of the Church were the Church's poor, but he spoke according to the usage of the word in his own time.

60

Without rashness we say that the keys of the Church, given by Christ's merit, are that treasure;

61

For it is clear that for the remission of penalties and of reserved cases, the power of the pope is of itself sufficient.

62

The true treasure of the Church is the Most Holy Gospel of the glory and the grace of God.

63

But this treasure is naturally most odious, for it makes the first to be last.

64

On the other hand, the treasure of indulgences is naturally most acceptable, for it makes the last to be first.

65

Therefore the treasures of the Gospel are nets with which they formerly were wont to fish for men of riches.

66

The treasures of the indulgences are nets with which they now fish for the riches of men.

67

The indulgences which the preachers cry as the "greatest graces" are known to be truly such, in so far as they promote gain.

68

Yet they are in truth the very smallest graces compared with the grace of God and the piety of the Cross.

69

Bishops and curates are bound to admit the commissaries of apostolic pardons, with all reverence.

70

But still more are they bound to strain all their eyes and attend with all their ears, lest these men preach their own dreams instead of the commission of the pope.

71

He who speaks against the truth of apostolic pardons, let him be anathema and accursed!

72

But he who guards against the lust and license of the pardon-preachers, let him be blessed!

73

The pope justly thunders against those who, by any art, contrive the injury of the traffic in pardons.

74

But much more does he intend to thunder against those who use the pretext of pardons to contrive the injury of holy love and truth.

75

To think the papal pardons so great that they could absolve a man even if he had committed an impossible sin and violated the Mother of God — this is madness.

76

We say, on the contrary, that the papal pardons are not able to remove the very least of venial sins, so far as its guilt is concerned.

77

It is said that even St. Peter, if he were now pope, could not bestow greater graces; this is blasphemy against St. Peter and against the pope.

78

We say, on the contrary, that even the present pope, and any pope at all, has greater graces at his disposal; to wit, the Gospel, powers, gifts of healing, etc., as it is written in I. Corinthians xii.

79

To say that the cross, emblazoned with the papal arms, which is set up [by the preachers of indulgences], is of equal worth with the Cross of Christ, is blasphemy.

80

The bishops, curates and theologians who allow such talk to be spread among the people, will have an account to render.

81

This unbridled preaching of pardons makes it no easy matter, even for learned men, to rescue the reverence due to the pope from slander, or even from the shrewd questionings of the laity.

82

To wit: — "Why does not the pope empty purgatory, for the sake of holy love and of the dire need of the souls that are there, if he redeems an infinite number of souls for the sake of miserable money with which to build a Church? The former reasons would be most just; the latter is most trivial."

83

Again: — "Why are mortuary
and anniversary masses for the
dead continued, and why does
he not return or permit the
withdrawal of the endowments
founded on their behalf, since
it is wrong to pray for the
redeemed?"

84

Again: — "What is this new piety of God and the pope, that for money they allow a man who is impious and their enemy to buy out of purgatory the pious soul of a friend of God, and do not rather, because of that pious and beloved soul's own need, free it for pure love's sake?"

85

Again: — "Why are the penitential canons long, since in actual fact and through disuse abrogated and dead, now satisfied by the granting of indulgences, as though they were still alive and in force?"

86

Again: — "Why does not the pope, whose wealth is to-day greater than the riches of the richest, build just this one church of St. Peter with his own money, rather than with the money of poor believers?"

87

Again: — "What is it that the pope remits, and what participation does he grant to those who, by perfect contrition, have a right to full remission and participation?"

88

Again: — "What greater blessing could come to the Church than if the pope were to do a hundred times a day what he now does once, and bestow on every believer these remissions and participations?"

89

"Since the pope, by his pardons, seeks the salvation of souls rather than money, why does he suspend the indulgences and pardons granted heretofore, since these have equal efficacy?"

90

To repress these arguments and scruples of the laity by force alone, and not to resolve them by giving reasons, is to expose the Church and the pope to the ridicule of their enemies, and to make Christians unhappy.

91

If, therefore, pardons were preached according to the spirit and mind of the pope, all these doubts would be readily resolved; nay, they would not exist.

92

Away, then, with all those prophets who say to the people of Christ, "Peace, peace," and there is no peace!

93

Blessed be all those prophets who say to the people of Christ, "Cross, cross," and there is no cross!

94

Christians are to be exhorted that they be diligent in following Christ, their Head, through penalties, deaths, and hell;

95

And thus be confident of entering into heaven rather through many tribulations, than through the assurance of peace.

END

FIRST DISPUTATION OF JOHANN TETZEL.

Attributed to Conrad Wimpina — 1517

In order that the truth may appear, and errors be suppressed, and, after due consideration, objections against Catholic truth be answered: brother Johann Tetzel, of the order of Preachers, Bachelor of Sacred Theology, and Inquisitor of heretical pravity, will sustain the subscribed propositions in the most distinguished univerisity at Frankfort-on-Oder.

To the praise of God for the defence of the Catholic faith; and for the honor of the Holy Apostolic See.

1. Our Lord Jesus Christ [wished to teach all] the sacraments of the new law, by which he wished all to be bound, after his passion and ascension, [2] and he wished to teach all before his passion by the most suitable proclamation.

3. Therefore he errs, whoever says that Christ, when he proclaimed "Repent ye," wished inward repentance and outward mortification of the flesh in such wise, [4] that he could not also teach or at the same time understand the sacrament of penance and its parts—confession and satisfaction—as obligatory. Nay, verily, it avails nothing even if inward penance works outward mortification unless confession and satisfaction are accompanied by deed and prayer. (1,2)*

5. This satisfaction (since God does not allow a transgression without a penalty) is made through penalty, or its equivalent in the divine acceptance.

6. What is imposed, either by the will of the priest or by canon, is sometimes enforced by divine justice here, or is remitted in purgatory. (4)

7. Just as no one is bound to repeat a confession, truly made,

---

* The numbers in parentheses at the end of this and other theses, indicate which of Luther's theses is being attacked by Johann's disputation.

for the same offenses, save in few cases; [8] And however useful it might be, nevertheless neither priest nor Pope can demand that it be repeated, [9] So one absolved is not bound to repeat for the same sins the outward satisfying penance, when once rightly performed. To command the contrary is to err. (3, 4.)

10. Notwithstanding, he is bound as long as he lives to grieve within, in conduct and disposition, and always to detest remitted sin, and not to live without fear concerning propitiation of sins.

11. This penalty, imposed on account of sins repented and confessed, the Pope can completely remit by means of indulgences; [12] Whether this has been imposed by him, or by the will of the priest, or by canon, or even is exacted by the divine justice; to deny this is to err. (5)

13. But although through indulgences every penalty in matters determined is remitted which is due for sins, so that it is vindicative of them; [14] he errs, nevertheless, who thinks that because of this the penalty is removed that is healthful and preservative, since the Jubilee* is not ordained contrary to this.

15. However truly and entirely any one may receive remission through indulgences—he who denies that this can be done in matters determined errs; [16] Nevertheless no one ought to intermit works of satisfaction as long as he lives, since they are curative of sins remaining, preservative from future sins and meritorious.

17. Just as the Mosaic sacraments are barren elements, neither removing guilt nor justifying: [18] So the Jewish priests have neither keys nor office [*characterem*] whence they can remit

---

* By Jubilee, here Tetzel is referring to the Pope Leo X's declaration of a plenary (full) indulgence, also refered to as *in forma Jubilaei.*

guilt.

19. But the Christian sacraments produce the grace they signify, and hence also justify those who receive them.

20. And Christians priests have the true office and keys, by which they can remit even guilt: [21] not only by approving and declaring, as the priests of the old law of Aaron did with regard to leprosy, [22] but also ministerially and instrumentally, and by orderly performing the thing itself by means of the sacrament. (6)

23. Nay, just as God has keys of authority, Christ of excellence, so the Christian priest has ministerial keys.

24. Whoso says, therefore, that the Pope, or even the least priest, has no power over guilt save in approving or declaring, errs. (6)

25. Nay, he errs who does not believe that the least Christian priest has more power in regard to sin than the whole synagogue of the Jews formerly had.

26. Why does he not err then, who thinks that Christ, so far as he has not bound his power to the sacraments, [27] cannot remit sins by the excellence of his key, and save a man, apart from sacerdotal confession, approbation or declaration? (7)

28. Although contempt, true or inferred, has rejected the sacrament, which not seldom happens in late repentance, [29] neither unexpected death nor necessity exempt from the severest punishment that follows.

30. Nevertheless, we must not despair concerning these, since the least contrition that can take place at the end of life, [31] suffices for the remission of sins and the changing of the eternal penalty to a temporal.

32. But seeing that, on account of deficiency of time, the most cruel punishments not infrequently befall those who have

died in such wise, [33] which are quickly remitted by plenary indulgences, such act foolishly as dissuade from buying confessional licenses.

34. Because of violence to a priest, penalties are imposed on the excommunicate, incendiaries, and incestuous, not alone after absolution, but sometimes after death; [35] on the one an oath not to repeat, on the other satisfaction—therefore he who denies that this can be done, errs. (10).

36. Not by sleeping bishops, but by chapters of the [canon] law, a priest is commanded to be discreet and pious, so that one confessed is sent to purgatory, [37] with the penalty of exile willingly received, rather than to hell as rejected. Who calls that "tares" therefore errs. (11).

38. Heretics, schismatics and traitors, are excommunicated after death, anathematized and exhumed. [39] Therefore, whoever says that those about to die pay all debts by death, and are not held by the canon law, errs. (13).

40. It is erroneous to say that souls about to be purified, who depart in grace and charity—which separates between the sons of the kingdom and those of perdition, and far more of despair—[41] are near despair; but rather [one should say] they are in firm hope of obtaining happiness. (14, 15).

42. He errs who says that it is not proved either by reason or Scripture, that the purified are beyond the state of merit. (18).

43. He errs who adds, that it is not proved how certain and secure they are of their happiness. Likewise he who says, [44] the souls about to be purified cannot be more certain of their salvation than we, and that we are most certain. (19).

45. He errs who says that the Pope does not mean by plenary remission the remission of all penalties, but only those imposed by himself. (20).

46. To say that the preachers of indulgences err when they declare that a man may be relieved of all penalty by the indulgence of the Pope and be saved, is an error. (21).

47. To say that the Pope can remit no penalty to souls in Purgatory which they ought to remove in this life according to the canons, is an error. (22).

48. He errs who says that only the most perfect can obtain pardons, and not also the perfect, the still more perfect, beginners and progressive. [49] Likewise also [whoever says that] not only the fully contrite but the impenitent [*attritos,* imperfectly penitent] and the contrite through confession [can obtain pardons.] (23).

50. He errs whoever says this can happen to very few, and not to most who do what the Jubilee requires. (24).

51. It is an error to assert that the Pope has no greater or more efficacious power over Purgatory, by imparting generally the Jubilee [i. e. its benefits] in form of intercession [52] than such or as great as any bishop or priest [*plebanus,* lit. country priest] has especially in his own diocese and parish. (25).

53. Even if the Pope have no power of the keys over Purgatory, he nevertheless has the authority to apply the Jubilee to them by way of intercession. (26).

54. To deny this power over Purgatory in the Pope, under the form of the key, is to contradict the truth and to err. (26).

55. For a soul to fly out, is for it to obtain the vision of God, which can be hindered by no interruption, [56] therefore he errs who says that the soul cannot fly out before the coin can jingle in the bottom of the chest. (27).

57. It is an error to find gain and avarice in public intercession, and not to seek the effect of purgation. (28).

58. It is a manifest error to doubt if all souls wish to be

redeemed, or being redeemed to escape Purgatory. (29).

59. With regard to conjectural security, as far as human weakness attains, it is an error [to hold] that no one is certain of obtaining pardon, even those who have done what the Jubilee requires. (30).

60. It is an error [to say] that only a few, and not most of those who fulfil the Jubilee requirements, obtain pardons. (31).

61. It is an error [to say] that one released through plenary pardon, according to the form of the decretal [*rescripti*], is not certain of his salvation just as if truly confessed and penitent. (32).

62. It is an error [to hold] that a man is not reconciled to God by papal indulgences duly acquired by every form, just as if truly penitent and confessed. (33).

63. It is an error [to teach men] not to look for pardoning grace, except for penalties of satisfaction imposed by man, and not also those imposed by the canon or divine justice. (34).

64. It is an error [to say] that it is not a Christian doctrine, that those who are about to buy confessional licenses or the Jubilee indulgence for their friends in purgatory can do these things without repentance. (35).

65. It is an error [to hold] that any Christian whatever, truly penitent, has quickly and completely plenary remission of penalty and guilt without indulgences. (36).

66. It is an error [to say] that any Christian whatever, whether living or dead, has a share in all benefits, and to the extent of an authoritative remission of sins. (37).

67. It is an error to hold that there is the same share in all benefits through charity as through the power of having

mediation.* (37).

68. Again, it is an error [to say], that there is the same share in all benefits for acquiring and increasing merits, as for giving satisfaction.

69. It is an error to say that the remission of the Pope and the share [in all benefits] are not to be despised only because declaration is made of the divine remission.

70. It is an error [to say] that it is very easy, only for the most learned theologians, and not also for those moderately versed, at once to exalt the ample effect of pardons and the necessity of true contrition. (39).

71. He errs who does not know that, instead of those satisfying penalties that contrition seeks, Christ's pardons impose compensatory penalties, but because they do not remit those that are medicative, contrition has the penalties that it loves continuing through the whole life. (40).

72. Works of charity avail more in obtaining merit, but plenary pardons more in quickly making satisfaction and obtaining total remission. He errs who does not know this, or does not believe it, and who teaches the people one and is silent about the other. (41).

73. Plenary indulgences avail more in making satisfaction and obtaining remission completely, quickly and remarkably, but works of charity avail more in obtaining merit, grace, and chiefly in increasing glory. He errs who does not think the Pope wishes the people to be so taught. (41).

---

* *applicationem,* (lit. clientship.) The *ius applicationis* was the right of a client to the protection of his patron. The transference of this idea to the doctrine of indulgences is obvious. Elsewhere in the theses the word is rendered "intervention" or "mediation."

74. But since plenary indulgence differs exceedingly [*secundum excedentia et excessa*] from particular works of mercy (as they are commonly called) ; he is guilty of signal presumption and error who teaches the people that the Pope wishes the purchase of pardons to be in no way compared with so-called works of mercy. (42).

75. Giving to the poor and lending to the needy is doing better as to the increase of merit; but buying pardons is better as to more speedy making satisfaction. He errs who teaches the people otherwise and leads them astray; likewise he who thinks that to buy pardons is not also a work of mercy. (43).

76. Although by pardons a man may first become freer from punishment, nevertheless, since the work by which they are bought becomes one of charity, he who buys becomes better in consequence of his internal devotion. He doubly errs who teaches the people otherwise. (44).

77. Spiritual alms are preferable to corporal and are more commonly given. Whence if one needs pardon, and cannot aid the poor without danger of want, he does far better by buying than by helping the poor, as said before. He who teaches the contrary, errs. (44).

78. Merit and extent of merits are generally approved according to the importance of works and the purpose of charity; therefore he deserves pardons more who obtains them from necessaries than [he who obtains them] from superfluities. Whence he doubly errs who teaches that any one sins in acquiring merit in this way. (46).

79. Although the buying of pardons has not been commanded, it is nevertheless the wisest course for those who need them. Whoever says the former and is silent about the latter, leads the people astray and errs. (47).

80. What need Leo more than others has of prayers for himself

can only be conjectured [*est divinare*]. But we are bound to pray for Pope Leo by the obligation of both human and divine law. [81] And since that is done as a matter of necessity, he errs who says that on account of it the Pope ought to grant indulgences. (48).

82. Unless faith, devotion, nay confidence, are cherished with regard to pardons, indulgences amount to nothing and are useless. Whoever says the contrary errs most seriously. (49).

83. Since the sums exacted for pardons under Leo are very small as compared with his predecessors, therefore he errs impiously who says that he is planning to build the church of St. Peter's with the flesh, skin and bones of his own sheep. (50).

84. Indulgences are useful to him who does what lies in him, and according to the tenor of the bulls, however it may happen that railers [*oblatrantes*, lit. barkers] err. [85]. Therefore it is a most abominable error to say that confidence in salvation through letters of pardon is vain, even if the Pope were to put his own soul in pawn for them. (52).

86. If the least bishop can impose silence on others, either while he himself wishes to preach, or to have some one preach before him; [87] it is a very grave error to say that the Pope is the enemy of the cross if he wishes to publish the Jubilee in a like manner. (53).

88. If the legends of the saints may without harm be read on their feast days at greater length than the gospel, one can continue to publish pardons an equal or longer time than the reading of the gospel. To say the contrary is to err doubly. (54).

89. It is an error [to say] the mind of the Pope is, that pardons should be celebrated with single bells, processions and ceremonies, the gospel with a hundred bells, processions and ceremonies. (55).

90. It is an error [to say] that the treasury of the Church, whence the Pope grants indulgences, is not sufficiently named or known. (56).

91. It is an error [to say] that the treasury of Christ is not the merits of Christ and the saints. (58).

92. It is an error [to say] that these work pardoning (that is, sufficient on the side of God), quick, and complete satisfaction, without the mediation of the Pope. (58).

93. [To say] that the treasure of the Church was the poor, in the time of St. Lawrence is an error. (59).

94. [To say] that the treasure of the Church is only the keys of the Church given by the merit of Christ, is an error. (60).

95. It is an error [to say] that the power of the Pope alone suffices for the remission of penalties, without intervention of the treasury of the Church, that is, of the merits of Christ. (61).

96. The gospel, the gift of healing, [and] the sacraments of pardon are alike called by the name of grace; to proclaim the one and neglect the other is to err. (62).

97. It is an error [to say] that the indulgences that preachers proclaim to be the greatest graces, are truly such as to promoting gain. (67).

98. Yea, [to teach] that the treasuries of indulgences are nets with which they fish for the riches of men, is a most impious error. (66).

99. And since a sin committed against the mother of Christ, however enormous, is less than if the same were committed against the Son, which is remissible by the express testimony of Christ, [100] therefore whoever says that such a sin cannot be remitted in the truly contrite by indulgences, is mad, raves and errs, against the text of the gospel and Christ himself. (75).

101. Moreover, to propose to the subcommissaries and preachers of pardons that if, by an impossibility, anyone should violate the ever virgin mother of God, they could absolve the same by the power of indulgences—it is clearer than light that the one so proposing against the evident truth, is moved by hatred and thirsts for the blood of his brethren. (75).

102. To lay down also in public propositions, that preachers of pardons (although never heard) overflow before the people with excess of words and consume [*proterrere*, lit. frighten away] more time in explaining pardons than in preaching the gospel, is to sow falsehoods heard from others and invented for truth, and he who quickly believes shows himself thereby to be fickle and errs grievously. (72, 54).

103. In fine, to lay down in public propositions, that preachers of pardons are so far wanting through their licentious preaching as to make it no easy task even for learned men to secure respect for the Pope from the questions of acute laymen, is, after first bringing contumely [contempt] upon the Pope, to flatter him and openly insinuate that all the rest have obtained safely [portum possidisse], and that he alone makes trouble, and in this to err exceedingly. (81).

104. It belongs to grace formally to remit guilt, effectively and chiefly by God, regularly (though insufficiently) by a pure man,* satisfactorily by Christ, instrumentally by the sacraments. Whoever therefore says the Pope cannot remit the least venial [sin] as to guilt, errs. (76).

105. He who denies that the same power belongs to Peter and all his Vicars, errs. Whoever thinks Peter has more power over pardons than Leo errs greatly, yea, blasphemes. (77).

---

* *homini puro;* or, this may mean, by a mere man, by man alone.

106. He errs who says just as he who adores the cross of Christ or any image whatsoever, as a thing and not as a sign, offers divine worship [*latria adorat*], likewise that the cross of Christ excels among however many others, as objects of adoration, and ought to be venerated more; nevertheless, he who offers divine worship to other things, and does not equally adore that [cross] represented also in the papal arms, is guilty of idolatry and error. (69).

//

Part of the foregoing theses were translated by Mr. John Keesee Goode, class of 1901, of the Crozer Theological Seminary. They have been revised, completed and annotated by Professor Vedder. The text of the theses may be found in Loeschern's *Vollstaendige Reformations-Actaund Documenta* (Leipzig, 1720, 3 vols.) 1:504sq., and in Luther's *Opera Latina* (Erlangen ed.) 27:294sq. Tetzel was never believed to be the author of these theses—though the composition of them does not seem to be beyond his very ordinary capacity—and their authorship has been very generally attributed to Conrad Wimpina, one of the leading teachers of the University at Frankfort-on-Oder. See Beard's *Martin Luther and the Reformation in Germany* (London 1889) p. 223sq.

SECOND DISPUTATION OF JOHANN TETZEL.

Brother Johann Tetzel, of the order of Preachers, Bachelor of Sacred Theology, and inquisitor of heretical pravity, will publicly and briefly defend and dispute the subscribed propositions, at the university of Frankfort-on-Oder, on a certain day that will be named at the earliest possible time : whoever ought to be censured as heretic, schismatic, obstinate, contumacious, erroneous, seditious, ill-expressing, rash and injurious, at the first look will be clearly seen in them.

To the praise of God and the honor of the Holy Apostolic See, in the year of our salvation, 1517.

1. Christians should be taught that, since the power of the Pope is supreme in the Church and was instituted by God alone, it can be restrained or increased by no mere man, nor by the whole world together, but by God only.

2. Christians should be taught that they are bound to render simple obedience to the Pope, who holds them all in his immediate jurisdiction, in respect to those things that pertain to the Christian religion and to his chair, if they are consonant with divine and natural law.

3. Christians should be taught that the Pope, by authority of his jurisdiction, is superior to the entire Catholic Church and its councils, and that they should humbly obey his statutes.

4. Christians should be taught that the Pope has the sole [power] of deciding those things that are of faith, and that he and no other may interpret the sense of Holy Scripture as to its meaning, and that he has [the power] to approve or disapprove all the words or works of others.

5. Christians should be taught that the judgment of the Pope, in those matters that are of faith and necessary to man's salvation, cannot err in the least.

6. Christians should be taught that even if the Pope should err in faith, concerning the things that are of faith, by holding a bad opinion, he will not err concerning those things that are of faith when he pronounces judgment upon them.[*]

7. Christians should be taught that the decisions of the Pope, which he publishes as to matters that are of faith, ought to have more weight in a cause than the decisions of any number of wise men regarding the doctrines [*opinionibus*] of the Scriptures.

8. Christians should be taught that the Pope deserves always and humbly to be honored by them, and not to be injured.

9. Christians should be taught that those who derogate from the honor and authority of the Pope, incur the penalty of the curse and the crime of treason [*laesae majestatis.*]

10. Christians should be taught that those who expose the Pope to jeers and slanders, are marked with the stain of heresy

---

[*] That is, the Pope may be a heretic privately, and as to his personal beliefs, yet in his official action as head of the Church he will be preserved by the Holy Spirit from error. This thesis anticipates with remarkable accuracy the treatment by modern theologians, as Hefele, of the case of Pope Honorius, who in 680 was anathematized by the Sixth Ecumenical Council for heretical views expressed in a letter to Sergius, Patriarch of Constantinople (Mansi, XI:631; Hefele, *History of Councils*, Eng. tr. V:167.) These views, not being spoken *ex cathedra*, as pastor and teacher of all Christians, are not regarded by Roman theologians as coming within the scone of the Vatican definition of infallibility (Schaff, *Creeds of Christendom*, II:270.)

and shut out from hope of the kingdom of heaven.

11. Christians should be taught that those who dishonor the Pope are punished with temporal disgrace, and also with the worst death and scandalous disorder.

12. Christians should be taught that the keys of the Church do not belong to the universal church, as the assembly of all believers is called, but to Peter and the Pope, and have been bestowed on all their successors and on all prelates to come, through derivation from them.

13. Christians should be taught that a general council cannot give plenary indulgence, nor other prelates of the Church, together or singly, but the Pope alone, who is the bridegroom of the Church universal.

14. Christians should be taught that no mortals can determine the truth and faith concerning the obtaining of indulgences— no, not even a general council, but the Pope alone, who has [the power] to render final judgment concerning catholic truth.

15. Christians should be taught that catholic truth is called universal truth, and that it ought to be believed by Christ's faithful ones, and that it contains nothing either of falsehood or of iniquity.

16. Christians should be taught that the Church holds many things as catholic truths, which are by no means contained in the same form of words in the canon of Holy Scripture of the Old and New Testaments.

17. Christians should be taught that the Church hold many things as catholic truths, which nevertheless arenot laid down as such either in the biblical canon or by earlier teachers.

18. Christians should be taught that all observances regarding matters of faith, defined by the decision of the Apostolic See,

are to be reckoned among catholic truths, although not found to be contained in the canon of Holy Scripture.

19. Christians should be taught that those things that teachers approved by the Church have positively handed down concerning the holding of the faith and the confuting of heretics, although they are not expressly contained in the canon of Holy Scripture—their writings of this character are nevertheless to be reckoned among catholic truths.

20. Christians should be taught that although certain truths may not be absolutely catholic, they none the less smack of catholic truth.*

21. Christians should be taught that all those smack of heresy, who say that no use of the cross of Christ should be made in the Churches.

22. Christians should be taught that those who cherish deliberate doubts concerning the faith should be most clearly condemned as heretics.

23. Christians should be taught that those who are ordained to holy orders for money may most clearly be called heretics.

24. Christians should be taught that all who interpret the Holy Scripture badly, and not as the sense of the Holy Spirit demands, by whom it has been written, may most justly be called heretics.

25. Christians should be taught that he must properly be called a heretic, who for the sake of temporal glory either originates or follows false and new doctrines.

26. Christians should be taught that all those are most justly

---

* The Roman Church still maintains this distinction between dogma, a doctrine that is of faith and must therefore be believed by all, and a pious opinion that may be believed by any and should be treated with respect by all.

called heretics who attempt to take away the privilege of the Roman Church, delivered by the highest head of all Churches.

27. Christians should be taught that, after the example of the blessed Ambrose, they ought to follow in all things as their master the Holy Roman Church, and not their own imaginings.

28. Christians should be taught that whosoever persistently defends his own perverse and depraved doctrine, against the rule of catholic truth, should be condemned as a heretic and be proclaimed such by all.

29. Christians should be taught that those who teach anything as certain, which cannot be validly proved either by reason or by authority, must be condemned as rash.

30. Christians should be taught that those who assert at any time what things are false, are to be held as in error.*

31. Christians should be taught that those who draw away any one of the faithful, or some notable person, should be condemned as injurious.

32. Christians should be taught that those who write propositions that furnish occasion of disaster to those who hear, whatever qualification may be added, are truly to be held, as if they published them absolutely and without qualification, to be causes of offence, sayers of evil, and offenders of pious ears, in so far as they seem to urge heretical propositions.

33. Christians should be taught that assertions of teachers that bring in schism among the people—as is that proposition: One should not obey a bad prelate or prince, or, One should not believe the Pope and his bulls—are by all means seditious.

34. Christians should be taught that all who originate false

---

* Because only the Pope had the right (according to Tetzel) to do this.

doctrines, and defend them persistently, should properly be condemned as heretics,

35. Christians should be taught that all who, in contempt of the divine law, are either inventors of persistent error or followers of another, who would rather be opponents of catholic truth than its subjects, should certainly be condemned as heretics.

36. Christians should be taught that all defenders of others' errors, err not alone as to that, but also make ready for others stumbling-blocks of error, and show that they should not only be held to be heretics but even archheretics.

37. Christians should be taught that those who originate new doctrines contrary to catholic truth, which they may be pertinacious to hold, and because of them depart from the common life, from either fickleness or perversity, because this proceeds from pride, which properly is the love of superiority,—even if they are not influenced by any desire of temporal advantage, they are nevertheless without doubt to be held as heretics.

38. Christians should be taught that those who adhere to the doctrines of scholars [*Magistrorum*], contrary to catholic truth, err obstinately, and sin in erring, and thereby come to be condemned as heretics.

39. Christians should be taught that those who deny any catholic truth whatsoever, which is published as catholic among all the faithful with whom they associate, and is publicly proclaimed by preachers of the word of God, are said to be obstinate in their error.

40. Christians should be taught that those who deny the assertions which they know to be contained in Holy Scripture or in the decision of the Church, must be condemned as obstinate in their heresy.

41. Christians should be taught that those who do not correct or amend their error, whenever it has been shown them in a lawful manner that their error opposes catholic truth, must be condemned as contumacious in their heresy.

42. Christians should be taught that they must be condemned as obstinate in their error, who, erring against the catholic faith and the decision of the Church, proudly refuse to submit themselves to the correction and amendment of him to whom the duty belongs.

43. Christians should be taught that those who have been reproved for some plain error against the faith, and refuse to be informed concerning the truth, are in error and should be proclaimed as obstinate in this sort of heresy.

44. Christians should be taught that those who protest in words, deeds or writings that they are not at all willing to revoke their heretical assertions, even if those whose duty it is should rain or hail excommunications against such opinions, are to be held as obstinate heretics, and are to be shunned by all.

45. Christians should be taught that those who invent and defend new errors in defence of heretical pravity, in as far as they are not ready to be corrected and to seek truth with careful solicitude, are certainly to be held as obstinate in their heresies.

46. Christians should be taught that those beneath the chief Pontiff, if they formally define a certain assertion as heretical or decide that it must be held, and impose it uponothersbecausetheydeemittobecatholic,—are to be held and proclaimed as obstinate heretics, one and all who agree with such decisions of theirs.

47. Christians should be taught that they obstinately err, who have the power to resist heretical pravity, and yet do not resist

it, and that by this course they themselves befriend the errors of heresy.*

48. Christians should be taught that those who defend the error of heretics and effect this by their own power, [should beware] lest they come into the hands of the judge to be tried, as excommunicates, and if they do not make satisfaction within a year, be held by their own law as infamous, who are also according to the chapters of the law terribly punished with many penalties, to the terror of all men.

49. Christians should be taught not to be influenced, in their faith about the authority of the Pope and his indulgences, by the boldness of obstinate heretics, for our pious Lord and God would not have permitted heretics to arise, except that Truth might appear more clear to faith by their arising, and we might by this means escape from irrational infancy; but they should rather continue credulous regarding the truth preached concerning the parts of penance and indulgences; through which constancy on their part in the aforesaid faith, the approbation of them by God may be made clear and evident to the whole world.

50. And so those who wish as much as they can to fill letters and books concerning the parts of penance (confession of the mouth and satisfaction by works, brought in and instituted by God and the gospel, and promulgated by Apostles, and approved and followed by the whole Church, and yet impugned by [my]** adversary unrighteously and irreligiously in his common speech, in so many articles), and concerning plenary indulgence and the power of the chief Roman Pontiff with regard to the same, and [wish] with a certain

---

* This thesis and the one following are evidently aimed at the Elector Frederick, of Saxony.
** The pronoun is evidently required, for the reference can be to nobody but Luther.

unrestrainable cheek [*fronte*] to preach publicly or dispute concerning them, to win favor for their writings, scatter them among the people and make them common throughout the world, or to speak impudently and by way of contempt concerning these very things, in corners or in part before men,—let them fear for themselves lest they fall upon the foregoing propositions, and through this expose themselves and others to the peril of damnation and of severe temporal disorder. For a beast that has touched the mountain shall be stoned.

//

The text of these theses may be found in Loeschern, 1 :5i7sq; also in Luther's *Opera Latina*, 27: 306—312. The debate thus challenged was actually held, January 21, 1518, at which time Tetzel was declared a Doctor of Theology (Beard, *Martin Luther*, p.223.)This second list of theses is a far more able document than the first; they set forth with a good deal of rude force the doctrines of the supremacy and infallibility of the Pope, as held in Luther's day by the advanced Roman theologians, and formally confirmed and made an article of faith in our own day by the Vatican Council.

FOR FURTHER READING

Martin Luther's 95 Theses — by Timothy J. Wengert

Historical Leaflets — from The Crozer Theological Seminary

The Legacy of Luther — Edited by R.C. Sproul and Stephen J. Nichols

Katharina and Martin Luther — by Michelle DeRusha

Here I Stand: A Life of Martin Luther — by Roland Bainton

The Real Martin Luther — by Josh Hamon

I hope you'll take a moment to check out my other works, including:

THE REAL
𝔐artin 𝔏uther

Read the first chapter free at therealmartinluther.com or from TheMinistryofWar.com.

As of this writing, about 2.2 billion people call themselves Christians. You would have a hard time finding something all of them agree on. Those differences can affect how we perceive our heroes of faith. We tend to only learn a small sliver about our heroes of faith. The good sliver.

The Real Martin Luther takes an honest look at this controversial historical figure. He's far more than the man behind the 95 Theses. With the help of more than 150 images, you can expect to smile, laugh and smirk while enjoying history that isn't dry or unnecessarily serious.

Did I mention you can get the first chapter free at therealmartinluther.com or theministryofwar.com?

The Ministry of War

uncommon books for uncommon geeks

www.ingramcontent.com/pod-product-compliance
Lightning Source LLC
Chambersburg PA
CBHW071907020426
42331CB00010B/2707